THE DEAD SNAIL DIARIES

Jamie McGarry was born in Norwich, in April 1988, and grew up in North Wales and Yorkshire. He attended university in Scarborough, earning a degree in English Literature and Culture, as well as founding a publishing label, Valley Press, in 2008. Perhaps unsurprisingly, this led to the release of several books by Jamie – including a novel, *The Waiting Game*, and two volumes of poetry, *What Do I Know Anyway?* and *Autopilot*. He currently lives in East Yorkshire, pursuing these bookish interests to his heart's content.

A slow-moving, brown-hued creature, Jamie regularly enjoys a leafy salad, and has (on occasion) been known to come out of his shell.

The Dead Snail Diaries

JAMIE MCGARRY

VALLEY

THE DEAD SNAIL DIARIES

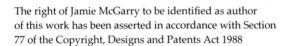

First published in 2011
by Valley Press
www.valleypressuk.com

Printed in England by Orbital Print,
Sittingbourne, Kent

The right of Jamie McGarry to be identified as author
of this work has been asserted in accordance with Section
77 of the Copyright, Designs and Patents Act 1988

ISBN: 978-0-9562519-9-2
IPN: VP0012

A CIP record for this book
is available from the British Library

www.valleypressuk.com/authors/jamiemcgarry
www.jamiemcgarry.com

9 8 7 6 5 4 3 2 1

for everyone
who feels
not quite far enough
from the ground

CONTENTS

Introduction

In May 2009 I stepped on a snail, and detailed my subsequent guilt in a poem (as was the style at the time), *The Haunting of Poet by Snail*. The next morning, however, I returned to the scene of the crime and discovered a tiny book – the snail's personal diary – as well as (perhaps more puzzlingly) a miniature outline in chalk.

Having quickly decoded the language of the diary (modern snailish), I discovered I had inadvertently crushed a writer of some ambition and literary· talent. The diary contained details of snail-kind's surprisingly advanced social systems and activities, as well as their often unhealthy relationship with slugs, a previously unheard seafaring legend, and some highly memorable puns.

Truly inspired, I set about translating the contents and adapting them into poetry – a work which I have presented here for your consideration. I hope you enjoy it, and please read slowly; I feel sure that's what he would have wanted.

J.M. / October 2010

The Haunting of Poet by Snail

Has it been four days now?
Must have been. Nearly a week
since I did the deed. It was dark,
and I was hurrying – I didn't see
his form, the path in front of me.
My careless size-ten shoe came down,
and crushed his hopes and dreams.

My stride stopped mid-step. Sickened
by that sound, the chilling crunch;
I saw him, when I lifted up.
A tragic mix of slime and shrapnel.

And now – although you'll doubt –
I swear he's back. I am the mollusc's
sole unfinished business
on this fast and brutal Earth.

You'll say it's in my head, if I report
that I can hear his death
in every mistimed gearshift,
every mouth devouring crisps.

But it's not my conscience doing this,
it's *him*. He's putting me through hell.
I hear, with every step I take,
the breaking of the tell-tale shell.

Last night, I thought I saw him,
bright and cold, in death.
Slowly sliding next to me,
and felt his tiny, ghostly breath.

'It was dark!' I scream. 'I was hurrying!'
His silence says it all. But still,
you don't believe me? Come on round,
see the trails across my walls...

and explain the vengeful holes
in my fridge-ridden, cellophaned lettuce.

A Love Poem: From Snail to Slug

God made us brown so we'd be hard
to spot upon his fertile soil,
to hide from the birds...which he made as well...
to cower, dodge, to postpone hell.

But slug does not hide, or flinch back.
His coat? Uncompromising BLACK.
He turns defence into attack.
Oh slug – oh glorious slug.

God gave us shells to weigh us down.
Without them, we would HURTLE round,
so common sense suggests. Who'd beat us,
across a distance of ten metres?

But slug, dear slug, you have the grace
to not rub freedom in our face,
to slow your stride to match our pace.
Oh slug – oh glorious slug.

God made us quiet, thoughtful, wait.
He taught us manners, and restraint.
He taught us not to stay out late,
we're model garden citizens.

But slug, he DEAFENS when he speaks!
He goes out seven nights a week!
Beer-swilling, hard-living, party beast.
Oh slug – oh glorious slug.

I'd sell my soul to be like him.
Vacate my shell, and dye my skin.
I'd go twice weekly to the gym,
if doing so would let me in

to doors in town that say 'slugs only.'
But slug accepts no fake, no phony.
I'll love, but I will never be
a slug – oh glorious slug.

SIGH

SLUG

Slug's Night Out

It starts with getting all done up –
in black, of course. Straighten the antenna.
Then off, for the usual night on the tiles,
on the Johnsons' new-found patio.

We're the cool kids round here. Tough as *fuck.*
'Ain't no insect gonna mess with us!'
When the rest are tucked up in their beds,
we rule this town. Back door to fence.

Some call us anti-social. (The Johnsons?)
They deride our slime-art. Describe it in
their high society, garden magazines
as 'disgusting, unsightly, abhorrent.'

They wouldn't know life if it bit them in the face.

Snails? Those garden geeks? That's rich.
They don't have half the charm we have.
I could take them any day, cool as.
Front end tied behind my back.

We don't touch the pellets – the hard stuff.
Salt. We're tough, but we ain't mad.
But we're all on the grass, and I once had this mate,
nibbled his way through a catnip plant.

We lost one last night, drowned himself
in a vat of lukewarm beer. It's sad,
but there's worse ways to bow out. My mother
warned us that we'd wind up dead...

But we'll all be dried up in the end,
so excuse us if we live till then.

The Snail Not Taken

after Robert Frost

Two snails diverged on a plank of wood,
it's not clear what they're parting for.
Some careless words, misunderstood,
have come between these souls; once good
but now approaching all-out war.

There's some dispute, about a leaf.
First claimed by one, and then the next.
Each so secure in their belief,
that the other should be called the thief,
the debate has lost all context.

Now, they race to split apart,
to get some distance from their foe.
Clearly, it was that, or start
to tear the other one apart.
I thought it best to help them go.

I plucked one from the right-hand side,
and placed it carefully on a fence.
Two snails diverged on wood, and I
I moved the one with regret in its eyes –
and hoped it would make a difference.

Diary of a Church Snail

after John Betjeman

Down here among the crimson robes
choir boys (and girls) wear, over clothes
there's a lunch-box that's no longer full,
and slime on '...bright and beautiful
all creatures great and small.' That's me.
At home in either category
(although I'm not a 'snail of cloth',
or affiliated with a god).
I'm not here for the food – that's clear –
those hymn books give me diarrhoea,
and as for bread and jam, they're worse
(why don't mankind bring veg to church?)
I know what you are thinking, all,
'at least there's harvest festival,'
but by the time *I'm* there, the vicar's
tidied up ahead of Christmas.

So why, you ask, am I still here?
A vestry-dweller, year on year?
Living off the dying flowers
the ladies drop by after-hours,
instead of carving out a gash
across the vicar's cabbage patch?
Well, I find it's camouflaging,
hiding out among the carving –
(my humble shell is rather good
at fitting in with sculpted wood).
Also, though perhaps surprising,
I find that I agree with Larkin;
though empty, obsolete, and cold
this place does wonders for my soul.

It used to be the case, at Christmas,
there'd be some extra visitors,
earthworms, centipedes, woodlice
(and even those too-smug church mice).
While I live here the whole year round
they'd only creep out of the ground
the once; towards the end of year
to grab themselves some Christmas cheer.
And now, not even that. Just me
and Reverend turn up regularly;
though he may well give up for good
once I lie static on the wood.
Drop by and see us – bring some flowers,
bring comfort to these Christian hours,
and note, though cold and thin, I stay;
when all the rest have run away.

The Hollow Snails

after T.S. Eliot

I.

We are the hollow snails.
We are the dead snails.
Our voices, now echoing wind
through empty shells. Alas!
No-one lays wreaths
made of the blooms
we loved in life,
now we lie dead upon the grass.

They say we have the look
of jam-less jar, of pageless book.
Shape without motion; protection
without life to protect. Remember us –
if at all – not as gaping holes,
not as spent vessels of good souls,
but only as the hollow snails.
The dead snails.

II.

We are the crushed snails.
We are the squashed snails.
Trampled underfoot,
by thoughtless poets
(such as Eliot).

We will live on in your dreams,
snails as tall as trees –
eyes on stalks, swinging
eyes you dare not meet.

You will hear our voices in the wind,
you will remember
our first, and final encounter

the damp patch on the patio
glinting in the sunlight
like a fading star.

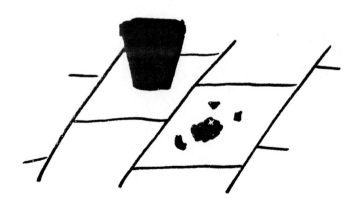

III.

We are the smashed snails.
We are the shattered snails.

Plucked from the prickly pear,
at five o'clock in the morning,
carried and dropped by gulls

from a great height

We fell. We were dead,
but for a second
between existence
and our end
we cast a shadow

from a height

You saw us
from a window,
between release
and our demise

from a great height

Between the motion
and the vision,
between death
and our descent
we cast a shadow

from a great height

on your heart

from a height

Not with a whimper but a bang.
Not with a whimper but a bang.

Snail Browner Than Ever

after Ted Hughes

Some species, I swear,
were made to suffer.

Noah didn't want them on the ark.
They tried to sneak on board one night,
but he saw their slime, the moonlit shine,
and threw them back into the dark.

They learned to swim –
which isn't easy,
when you've only got one foot.

They don't remember Eden,
HE doesn't remember THEM.
They must have come from somewhere,
but how, and where, and when...

They tried to give sweet Mary
a ride to Bethlehem!
They got themselves assembled, but
he'd been crucified by then.

And now, millennia later,
their rejection is complete.
The world grows ever upwards,
without glancing at its feet,

at the snails, still down there,
browner than ever –

flying their slippery flag
of surrender.

Snail Goes Speed Dating

*'The garden snail's courtship dance can last anywhere
from two to twelve hours...it concludes with the snails
firing a calcified 'love dart' at their partners, a kind of
tiny cupid's arrow.'*

Love does not move quickly.
Not for snails. Our pace is glacial.
Even mutual love at first sight
cannot be consummated
for several minutes, 'till
we slide into close contact.

'They rushed into each other's arms...'
Not quite. While aiming to collide
most snails exhaust all conversation,
find out each other's affectations,
become a bit resentful, even...
and when they reach a mating distance
just glare and slide right by.

A single red rose is a buffet.
A daisy? Eaten on the way.
Snail dating is an uphill climb,
snail dating is a loser's game,
so imagine, if you please, how poorly
we fare now they've added 'speed' to the name.

Slug, though, somehow always great.
He smirked when I asked for his secret
(since in truth, I *do* want a mate...)
'Snaily, dude, no worries!
You'll have noticed how we're pushed for time?'

(I had. I'd struggled to reach one
before the buzzer moved us on.)
'My secret comes in stunning rhyme,
with *pre-perfected chat-up lines.*'
I didn't look convinced. 'Just listen.
These lines will make your mate's skin glisten.'

Hey baby. Want to win my heart?
Come here and calcify my dart...

I'm your Prince Charming, Cinderella.
Let's tangle up our four antenna...

Let's cross our gleaming paths of slime,
along the short path back to mine...

'A little *blue*, Slug.' 'There's no harm in
having fun! They find it charming!'
He winked. 'You'll see. Before the morrow,
under the Johnson's new wheelbarrow...'
'That's quite enough.' '...ol' Slug
will have been stuck with Cupid's arrow.'

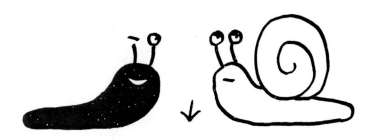

Ugh. What is it that he's eating?
I can't work out these foolish snails
who have a deep-set love of slugs,
who hanker after shell-less tails.
Snail dating's tricky just with us,
without competing with the slugs.
Snail dating's hopeless, doomed to crack
if slug-kind hoovers up the pack...

Another thing. You can't rely
on who's a gal and who's a guy.
My first 'speed date' looked like success
'till I went to compliment her dress
and found she'd somehow changed her sex –
HE barked at me in bass tones: 'NEXT!'
Oh, molluscs. What did I expect?

I slithered home alone that night.
No 'ticks'. A garden pest.

I dodged the slug's pre-claimed wheelbarrow,
and in the process, drowned my sorrows
with a shortcut through the garden pond,
and thought how best I might respond.

Floating upside down in murk
I watched my dark reflection,
a sad and wonky echo, 'till
the gloom began to lessen...

I saw flowers, eaten, at a wedding.
My lover, met in one chance meeting,
my children, bright and shiny-shelled –
with eyes on stalks, this snail beheld
what must have been the perfect course,
all love, no chaos or divorce;
the details of a happy future
in a mirror held above the water.

I spun the right-way up, broke through
the shining surface of the pond,
but found the things I saw there, gone.
And cried for I remained, still, one.

But later, in cold morning light
I thought that what I saw was life,
the opportunities still mine,
if I could only realise
that love, like all things grand, takes *time*...

and that, at least, I have
in great supply.

A Snail's Advice to His Son

after Gervase Phinn

Always keep your shell clean, son.
It shows the world you care.
Hold your antenna straight and proud
and pointing in the air.

Trail your slime in crisp, clean lines
in parallel to walls,
stick to grass where dogs are banned
(and games involving balls).

If you must steal mankind's veg
wait till they're not around.
Steer well clear of allotments ('least
until the sun's gone down).

Although you may not have one, son,
be sure to chance your arm.
Confronted by a gang of slugs,
let your response be calm.

Keep your head in times of stress
(inside your shell, if poss.)
When I am gone, just carry on.
Smile, despite your loss.

Keep that sense of patience,
never let your stride be rushed;
and don't take life too seriously, son
for few survive uncrushed.

Pringleplanks: The Railway Snail

from 'Old Possum's Book of Sensible Snails', 1937

There's a holler most irate, at 11:38
when the Snail Mail's ready to up anchor,
saying 'Pringle where is Pringle, *is he flirting with a
    thimble?*
We're screwed without that slimy little chancer!'
All the guards and the commuters and the *Ticket-Max*
    computers
search for him online and, well, on line
crying 'Pringle where is Pringle? He's the one and
    only thing'll
stop the nation's post from leaving here on time!'
By 11:43 those involved (hysterically)
start to root through luggage for their mollusc mascot.
Then Pringle will resurface, just in time to start his
    service
wearing an expression that says: '...what?'
   Then he gives one wave of his tiny prongs
    and the signal flicks to green,
    and we're off at last (though not all *that* fast)
    for what's North of Aberdeen.

You'll be shocked to understand that a snail is in
    command
of the train that runs this vital night-time route,
but relax, it's all been planned – Pringle has the job in
    hand
(and besides, you must admit he's rather cute).
While there are those who disparage, claim he can't
    traverse one carriage
in the time it takes from King's Cross up to Glasgow,
they've got their wires crossed – Pringle's job is
    keeping watch;
eyes frontwards, focused on the track below.
Should you venture down to meet him, he will nod a
    quiet greeting,
but turn, as always, to his crucial role.
Never take the snail for granted – he's figurehead, a
    standard;
he signals when you've passed Hadrian's Wall.
    'This is the Night Snail, crossing the border!'
        Pringle seems to say
    (but we've no time for poor old Auden,
        only one spoof poem today).

Now the journey's halfway done, you can almost see the
    sun
rising somewhere to the East of Holy Island,
and though you'll hear an 'ahh' running up and down
    your car
the snail that saw it first will keep his silence.
His fellow train employees like to see him and swap
    stories,
and agree that Pringle helps to start their day;
when they board at Edinburgh, the new shift's delight is
    thorough
and the shout with which they greet him is 'HOORAY!'
In fact, he's so revered that, not only is he cheered
they've given him a share of company stock,
and at Christmas (though ridiculous, for tradesmen so
    meticulous)
they're known to let young Pringle run the signal box.
    But if you return to your cosy seat,
      and think this all seems insane –
    you ought to reflect, upon passing each station
    that you are protected from most vegetation;
    there's no-one so fine spotting leaves on the line
      as the *Snail of the Railway Train!*

All he needs when feeling peckish is a tiny piece of
    lettuce
and a shot-glass full of water lasts all night,
though a teaspoon of mild beer keeps the lookout in
    good cheer
(provide that, and you'll have a friend for life).
You were sleeping outside York, and so you never
    thought
that a snail had warned the driver of a cow;
but the pilots all know Pringle, and have learnt his set
    of signals,
that him waving his antenna means 'SLOW DOWN!'
When you reach your destination, out upon the final
    station
you'll see Pringle, standing solo, with a smile.
You should give a nod of thanks – for you've rode a
    thousand tracks,
and it's Pringleplanks who helped you all the while.
    Then he stands, at the front of his slimy trail,
        waving feelers once again;
    saying: 'now you know who put the "snail" *into*
        "mail" –
    'twas the *Snail of the Railway Train.*'

Einstein's Snail

Einstein had a theory
that when travelling at speed,
time would pass much faster
than it seemed –

while for those who travel slowly
it would still feel very long,
and he had a snail to tell him
he weren't wrong.

In Search of the Great Green Sea Snail

ONE: CAPTAIN MAX (FORMERLY PHIL)

Your oft-praised human goals
will be the end of all of us;
man and beast, snail and slug,
one day you'll surely screw it up.

I knew a human once, thought great,
was with him when he met his fate,
and now I come to tell the tale –
like Moby Dick, except with snails.

Maximus, he called himself
(though one day, hidden on a shelf
I found a copy of his will –
turns out his name was really Phil).

His mission, now passed into myth
was track down (if it did exist)
the Great Green Sea Snail, ancient song
suggests could be a half-mile long,

and ship it back to England. He'd
drag it, caged, to Sotheby's;
and if no-one should make the purchase
he'd sell it to the French, for burgers.

And me – just for the sake of speed –
he found me chewing on a leaf,
and as I wasn't properly stuck
he took me on the trip. For luck.

TWO: ACROSS THE SEA

The ship was cheered, the harbour cleared,
the day the *Treader* disappeared
in densest fog, which choked the air;
Max didn't spot the omen there.

I found life on that ghastly cruiser
ugly (well, at least the crew were).
A reluctant crewman, I suspected
most were coastguard who'd defected,

or just pirates, who'd decided
they no longer got excited
at the prospect of more looting;
so had switched to mollusc shooting.

I tried to keep well out of sight
when Max doled out the rum at night,
in fear they'd number my six sides
and use me as a makeshift dice;

I tried to hide out in the day
in case they hooked me up as bait
(as fish just off the coast of Wales
are deeply fond of juicy snails).

Frankly, I was most aggrieved
at having been brought out to sea,
and shouted (though outside their hearing)
'I don't remember volunteering!'

I tried to raise this with the Captain
but he was far too busy laughing,
full of glee at what he'd do
once his prize snail slid into view.

I became still more enflamed with woe
when Max picked up his wife's crossbow
she'd given him for luck, and shot
a cheery passing albatross –

I paced the deck (as best I could)
convinced this portent was not good;
Max and his crew ignored my hunch,
and had the tross' wings for lunch.

THREE: THE CHASE

After weeks of sailing senseless
the crew were fast becoming restless,
suspecting that the Great Green Snail
was just a strangely-shapen whale;

when the lad up in the sparrow's nest
flapped as if he'd been possessed,
waving Westwards with both hands
crying out 'IT'S LAND, SIR, LAND!'

The Captain was extremely pleased
so (having packed his eight CDs)
he left the crew to dice and fishing,
and took me on an expedition.

A desert island's what we found,
standard issue – sandy, round.
An island which, if asked, I'd say
had been attacked with PVA.

'This isn't glue,' said canny Max,
'There's only one beast makes these tracks,
we're literally ON the trail
of the legendary *Great Green Snail*!'

We left the island then, forthwith,
and once returned on board the ship,
Max stationed me to starboard side
at water's edge, to see if I

could hear the sea-snail's famous song.
(It seems I had been brought along
not for luck, or cunning strength
but hope our waves were similar length).

The crew looked on all through that day
while I thought of what best to say,
and how to say it – a form of speaking
that could dissuade a human being –

when I heard the sweetest string of notes
a vocal, bass, to soothe the soul,
and saw below me, 'midst the brine
a shape that looked a lot like mine.

I knew at once it would be cruel
to lead these men to nature's jewel,
so shouted at that emerald shape:
'THEY MEAN YOU HARM! YOU MUST ESCAPE!'

But she could not quite hear my shout,
so swam on up to check it out –
the Great Green Sea Snail pierced the surface.
My fault! My traitorous disservice!

The sudden sight had shocked the crew
who stood, slack-jawed, without a clue;
eye-contact with their Great Green prey
had taken their resolve away.

'Do something!' Shouted Max, until
the cabin boy (with zero skill
in shooting *or* in life) did shiver,
and caught his finger on the trigger.

The hot lead pinged off Great Green's shell,
a slight she seemed to take quite well –
or would have done, if Max's crew
had not all blindly followed suit.

The volley of ballistics seemed
to wake the Sea Snail from her dream,
through narrowed eyes our victim peered
and then – in seconds – disappeared.

'We've lost her!' Max exclaimed. Not true.
We felt the ship begin to move,
the water round our borders swirled,
while seamen screamed like little girls...

I hurried up the starboard side,
confounded by the darkened sky
and growing winds, and sudden rain –
a change I still cannot explain.

FOUR: SILENCE

The ship was carried far off course,
by winds the Sea Snail made Gale Force;
we hid below-decks, rode it out,
kept all the hatches battened down.

By now, my general consternation
at being in this situation
had turned to outright rage. Alas,
I couldn't take it out on Max --

I couldn't tell him how I felt
about the hand that he had dealt
this garden creature; human speech
remained beyond my humble reach.

One day the storm-front finally died,
so Max and co. stepped out, to find
on decks where they'd once strolled with ease,
they couldn't feel the slightest breeze.

Stranded, now. Becalmed. Of course,
not only were we far off course,
they'd used all petrol in the storm
to keep their sea-pyjamas warm.

But Max refused to back down *now.*
'I bet the Sea Snail's still around!
If I know her malicious mind,
she'll stick around to watch us die.'

So underneath both sun and moon
the crew stood poised with their harpoon
singing out – the criminals –
'if I could talk to the animals...'

But days turned into weeks, and still
the water lay completely still,
while Max (with admirable will)
stayed focused, ready for the kill.

The crew were looking somewhat glum
(not least since they'd run out of rum)
they'd water, but no drop to drink;
they'd gin, but hadn't brought the tonic.

I slept through all this consternation,
and caught up on some hibernation –
but woke from my much-needed sleep
on sensing tremors from the deep.

The crew thought their despair was over.
'We'll soon be safely back in Dover!'
Convinced the ship's renewed momentum
was from a breeze that God had sent 'em.

I tried a warning – but, too late.
No longer satisfied to wait,
the Sea Snail burst out from the blue,
and smashed the *Treader* clean in two.

'Don't panic!' Cried the Captain. 'We
need not fall dead into the sea!
We still can make the homeward trip
so long as we have half a ship!'

SMASH! The Snail emerged again,
and cleft the ship's two halves in twain,
at which Max re-affirmed his order
replacing the word 'half' with 'quarter'.

Devoted, still, to his doomed cause
the Captain grabbed a splintered oar,
and cried: 'Come back then! One more round!
We'll see just *who* is going down!'

At which there was a chilling rumble,
which caused the last few crew to tumble
into the waves (which claimed their lives).
I braced myself for *my* demise,

as Sea Snail surged from lowest reaches
and dashed the *Treader* into pieces.
She struck the ship again, again,
'till only splinters did remain.

I floundered in the crashing surf,
but vaguely managed to observe
the Great Green Sea Snail's head, receded,
regretful that this act was needed.

I saw her blink, shake off the woe,
prepare herself to dive below –
until she spotted one survivor,
and so (with all that spare saliva)

the Sea Snail swiftly doubled back
and had herself a post-war snack;
she didn't leave a lone spectator,
she swallowed Max (and your narrator).

49

FIVE: JONAH

On waking up inside the snail
I feared that we might not prevail;
as science now claims, uncontested,
the belly's where things get digested.

But lying there, Max reconsidered
the course that led him to these innards,
and spoke (at last) of his beginning,
of days when fortune still was with him.

When Max was Phil, and young, he spent
his days at large in rural Kent;
before his mind had time to harden,
he lived his life out in the garden.

His parents were organic folk,
but sadly, young Phil's heart was broke
when they both died from driving, drinking
(*not* from snails, as I was thinking).

With no relations, Phil left pretty
rural Kent for life mid-city;
assigned to live with other waifs
in council buildings, low on space.

But Phil refused to quit just yet,
the rules he chose to circumvent –
he saved his pennies, bought some seeds,
and filled his room with bright green leaves.

One day, there came some thrilling news;
a family who, when asked to choose
a child from his home's vast supply
had (just this once) not passed him by.

He spent the week before their meeting
pruning, watering and weeding
(and kept his window open wide
to let some half-fresh air inside).

He met the couple in the lobby,
conversed about his favourite hobby,
invited them to see his room;
his great creations, out in bloom.

(By now engrossed, I held my breath
suspecting what would happen next;
that what the couple went to see
meant Max might have it in for me.)

Sure enough, behind the door,
was Phil's formation, bright no more.
A sight straight from a horror scene –
it seemed a gang of *snails* had been.

Poor Phil could not explain his loss.
The family promptly brushed him off,
and he grew up leaf-free, alone;
convinced snail-kind had stole his home.

In later years, he turned his rage
to help design a product range;
he named his company PEST KILL MAX
and changed his name to match the packs.

'And so,' Max finished, 'understand
just why it was I always planned
at journey's end to squash *you* flat –
but now I can't do even that.'

(The positions we held in the tube
did not allow his legs to move;
all Max could do was softly cry
and wish all mollusc-kind would die.)

That's tragic, came a sudden voice
(though Max did not hear any noise.
I guessed, since I alone heard speech,
our host spoke through telepathy).

Yes... hi! I'm sorry 'bout this greeting
so soon after you both got eaten.
But snail, please ask... I'd like it solved,
just how I came to be involved.

'But...I can't speak!' I said. Aloud.
Poor Max's eyes popped halfway out.
I have the power to grant you speech,
now ask him why he hunted ME!

'She says, er...why did you pursue
the Great Green Sea Snail's trail of glue?
I mean, come on, you can't believe
that it was *her* who ate your leaves...'

Max, shocked by this sudden query,
replied with answer and a theory:
'It just seemed like the thing to do!
The Sea Snail's speaking using you?'

'The good is what you're angry at,'
I said. 'And yeah, Great Green said that.'
Max spoke again: 'I want her dead,
because she's snail-kind's figurehead!'

'Her race, who chewed my childhood leaves,
left ship and crewmen, lost at sea
to drown beneath the salty swell.
And now she's eaten me as well!'

Oh Max, she answered, *all must eat.*
But unlike you, the only meat
that I particularly devour
is that of the sea-cauliflower.

Snails eat plants, it's what we do!
It doesn't mean we're after you,
the flora in young Phil's display
helped some young snail live one more day.

'Wait a sec!' I said. 'Hang on.
Max – can I ask just how long
you left the room, that fateful night
you say the snail-gang ruined your life?'

'Er...fifteen minutes, tops.' He frowned,
and more so when I gasped, aloud.
Soon Sea Snail made the same deduction:
You smart oesophageal obstruction!

'It takes us hours to move one metre!
It's our most famed, distinctive feature!
Don't you see just what this means?
It *wasn't us* who ate your dreams!'

Max's mouth fell open wide.
His eyes stared at the Snail's insides,
but focused somewhere far beyond –
the past. Young Phil had got it wrong.

As Max let out a single tear,
Great Green chipped in: *You're no use here.
Take notice of my cousin's point –
go treat us well! Don't disappoint!*

And then, as sudden as we came
inside the Snail, we left again
(though I would hesitate to guess
which orifice released her guests).

SIX: JOLLY OLD SAINT PHIL (FORMERLY MAX)

Though cast once more into the waves
both man and snail were quickly saved –
I used my newfound 'magic throat'
to hail a passing fishing boat.

We didn't speak much, sailing back.
This was a new, more thoughtful Max;
and though I'd kept the power of speech
no apt remarks occurred to me.

(Plus, if I was overheard,
the sailors may have been disturbed;
I wanted all their concentration
fixed on tasks of navigation.)

Once safely back upon the shore
it seemed clear Max had been reformed;
he set me free, and made it plain
he'd never harm a snail again

(but plotted vengeance on the head
of the boy that family picked instead,
whose hands – now Phil brought him to mind –
were oddly *green* to wave goodbye).

No sooner than he'd said 'hello'
he bought his wife a new crossbow;
and on some sunset-smothered hill
he whispered to her: 'call me Phil'...

and filled with newfound glee, next day,
they bought a house out rural way,
with a garden you might call 'exquisite';
in part fenced off, so snails could visit.

And me? My talent did not fade,
in fact, I learnt to conversate
more than you lot with each other;
though mostly I choose not to bother.

Except... to stop the world forgetting,
I do a turn at fêtes and weddings;
telling guests this haunting story
of Max, and his mad quest for glory,

of how the Sea Snail changed his mind,
of how our mollusc brains (combined)
restored the sense to hateful Max
by just restating simple facts;

of how the sailor ceased to quarrel
when life revealed this simple moral:
'He prayeth well who loveth well
both man and bird and beast... and *snail*.'

Former Self

₁'

₁ondering if we pass it on
ₐr, or house –
 ₑₒₜₕ. Also, like clothes.

So 'detached, one careful owner,
size sixteen.' I had a lovely lady
hermit crab round yesterday,
looking to downsize for retirement.
'The kids have all grown up, moved out,'
she said, though she wasn't married.
I don't judge. I showed her the spiral staircase,
the games room, upstairs loo;
let her know I'd a family of woodlice
coming round later. Asked if she liked lettuce
at all, by way of conversation. You must
make an effort – plus, I was nervous.
It's like showing someone round your heart,
or a part of your body... that one
particularly.
                But it *is* strange. This is the place
I used to retreat to, when I needed
to feel safe – where I could really
be myself, you know? Contents just so,
everything perfect. Hard to let go. Anyway,
she told me she's more into seaweed.

Her offer wasn't quite what I wanted.
I've been eyeing up a yellow number
two houses along... nice bit of moss
round the doorway, like something
from childhood. Currently used

for decorative purposes, I assume. Sits
in a flower bed, and I've not seen it move.
Yes, I'll be happy there, once I shift
this old weight from my back,
once I clear out the attic. And yet –
my shell has been good to me;
seen me through all weathers,
no trouble from predators,
my choice of neighbours.
And when I curled up at night
inside, I knew I was home...
                                    Oh,
I'm fine. This is just me, droning on,
when I'm sure you have somewhere to go.

But if you're ever in need of a paperweight,
or an interesting ornament –
let me know.

A Snail at the Races

Fast Fred. Speedy Sam. Gatling-Gun Gus.
The irony's not lost on *any* of us

(except 'Schnell Shell', whose fierce German pride
keeps him from seeing the humorous side).

You've got to laugh. We spend our weeks in tanks
chasing each leaf that gets dropped in (thanks!)

which passes for training, which keeps us in shape
for the day the leaf serves as a finishing tape.

Some moan at this lifestyle. Not me. I rejoice,
remind them (like all athletes) we have a choice;

when called on to race we could simply play dead,
be released – take our chance with the songbirds instead.

They shut up, after that. So we race, twice a month
and the winner gets two weeks of feeling triumphant –

from the centres of circles, we race to the edges,
on the flat ('till they learn to grow round bonsai hedges).

Old Schnell doesn't speak on the days we go racing
for fear it will harm his intense concentration,

while Gus never stops motivational chanting,
to work himself up for his take-off (and landing).

I don't strain to win, but I aim to come close.
I try, lest I find myself spread on French toast,

and that's all they want, really. Effort. No tricks.
There's no need for pressure in *our* Olympics,

and I'm proud to report we've no problems with drugs
(for that sort of thing you should go watch the slugs)

the sole substance abused in the snail-racing pack
is the Tipp-ex they're using to number our backs.

And they're off. There are times when this feels like a joke,
when they're starting our races with *READY – SET – SLOW!*

but I look up at faces, as we start to shift
and see humans who care more than they would admit.

We go now to snail racing, streamed live from Congham.
Make yourselves comfy, this could be a long 'un...

The groundsman's been working all night on these pitches,
refining the radius to match fourteen inches,

dampening the surface to ensure a smooth glide,
and rolling – to him, it's a matter of pride.

The pace has been set now, we're one minute in
and all off the line! The fight truly begins

as we pick up some speed (though you'd not say we 'tear')
with announcer proclaiming each millimetre –

and it's Fast Fred in front at this mid-distance stage
with Schnell Shell trailing last, perhaps showing his age?

but Dart Derek is coming on strong to the North
with a roar from the crowd who are keen to support

that mollusc celebrity! His lithe slimy form
cuts through the air like a knife (slightly warm)

oh and Fred's now in front by a single antenna
just minutes from being remembered forever...

or at least, till the next race, which *feels* like forever.
The last race was won by one 'Tearaway Trevor'

but he was so winded from that great exertion,
he's passed on this meeting to go on vacation.

Dart Derek now slowing as we near the finish,
his gastropod stride starting...yes...to diminish,

while Gus, out of nowhere, is pushing ahead
setting his sights on the club's flowerbed,

but Schnell Shell is back out of nowhere! His eyes
are pointing straight forwards, transfixed on the prize,

he paced himself early on, we overlooked him,
but wait! Speedy Sam's coming round to obstruct him!

A clear violation of snail racing rules,
he may face beheading with gardening tools!

He's joking, but still, I'm not slightly amused
at this reference to commonplace mollusc abuse.

Of course, there aren't rules. It is widely agreed
such laws would be pointless, as snails cannot read...

(so they think). *Oh, incredible! Four cross the line –*
in three minutes thirty, a blistering time!

The scene here resembles that advert from Guinness,
the race has developed a true photo finish!

He says that, but really, they have time to fetch
the resident artist with his charcoal sketch.

Who wins doesn't matter, they've all done their bit.
Myself, I was content with finishing fifth,

what matters is, unlike most base earthly creatures
us snails have a place in world sport's upper reaches.

See, horses have jockeys... just us and humanity
(and possibly dogs) are allowed to compete

against one another, *man-to-man*, if you will;
and know that it's happening. This makes us *brill*.

We do this not just to keep safe, to keep housed,
but to keep snail-kind's image up, spread it around

that snails are worth keeping, that snails can be stars!
The glory we race for is not really ours,

who wins doesn't matter; we all win, each time.
We race to show everyone how snails can shine,

and we race on the promise that, if we're all good,
they'll let us retire – and be put out to stud.

coda

One day a snail saw Usain Bolt
run a hundred in nine-point-two –
and I swear that it muttered: 'I could do that.'
'I just don't *want* to.'

A Snail of Two Cities

'It was the best of times...
...it is a far, far better rest I go to.'

From Liverpool to Londonderry
I 'barnacled' it on the ferry.

From Newcastle to Whitley Bay
I hid amidst a large toupée.

From Bath to Weston-Super-Mare
I clutched a shoe to get me there.

From Middlesbrough to Holyhead
I rode as keepsake, playing dead.

One day I'll die for real, they say.
'Snails weren't meant to live this way!'

But I explain I'm well prepared
for the day my life cannot be spared,

as on the day we don't recover
we move from one place to another –

for, as times go, I've had the best;
to be only bettered by the rest.

Snail Attends a Beauty Contest

'Mirror, mirror, on the wall...
who's the fairest snail of all?'

'Mirrors can't talk,' Snail reminded his friend,
gliding past her in the hall.

'But *I* shall surely win!' She said.
'Have you seen my gleaming, varnished shell?'

'Have you seen my skin? So soft, and moist...
and my act's not bad as well.'

(Inside, Snail sighed. He'd only come
because he'd nothing better on.)

'You will do fine,' he said, and smiled.
'I'll see you when you're done.'

After the woodlice's opening number,
the contestants took to the stage

which being the one at the Royal Albert Hall,
took something quite close to an age.

Snails from all over went gliding around,
waving their prongs with great pride,

while our Snail, not one of the colourful ones,
just quietly watched from the side.

'Look at me!' Squealed his friend. 'I'm a goddess!'
'The pride of the gastropod race!'

The judges looked on, slowly shaking their heads,
disgruntlement writ on their face.

'Stop everything,' ordered the one at the end.
'This is not what we're after at all.'

'Your egos are out of proportion,
for creatures so slimy and small.'

'Showiness, attitude? It's not the snail way.
We've got this far being more chaste...'

'We're supposed to be sensible, dignified, grey;
your actions are simply bad taste.'

'Now him at the side...' said the judge, pointing wide.
'He knows what a snail ought to be.'

(Snail woke with a start, from a dream about art,
and thought 'is he talking to me?')

'Just watching, and keeping his thoughts to himself,
restrained, and impeccably wise.'

'Come over here son, step onto those boards...
let the crowd see you claiming first prize!'

Chuffed to his heart, Snail slithered across,
while the rest thought on what had been spoken.

He collected the trophy, and saw what it was –
a fifteen-pounds Waterstone's token.

A Snail Says

A cow says *moo!*
A sheep says *baa!*
A snake says *hiss!*

A dog says *woof!*
A cat says *miaow!*
A bird says *squark!*

A mouse says *squeak!*
A pig says *oink!*
A frog says *croak!*

A person says EH ALRIGHT SANDRA I WAS
JUST DOWN THE CORNER SHOP AFTER
TEN BENSON AND THE MANAGER WAS
ALL LET'S SEE SOME IDENTIFICATION
AND I WAS LIKE ARE YOU KIDDING AND
HE SAYS FRAID NOT SO I SAYS I'M
TWENTY THREE MATE AND HE SAYS
WELL YOU DON'T LOOK IT SO I SAID JUST
GIVE US THE FAGS BUT HE DIDN'T SO I
GOT SOME OFF DARREN

A snail says...

Gandhi's Snail

Pacifist? Aggression-less,
non-violent protest?
We got all that covered.
You heard it here first –

Mahatma G. grew up
a true teenage rebel,
'till he met his first snail
and his views were reversed.

Snail vs. the French

There's gastropods in a gastro-pub
in a country not that far from us –
the French! Oh yes, I'll tell the tale
of how *they* see the humble snail.

The French (god bless them) seem to have
a love of eating things they've found.
They saw a slimy, shell-shod thing
that slowly slid along the ground –

and thought 'that must be good to eat!'
(Who else would ever make that jump?)
I wonder what we've done to them,
that makes them make a meal of us?

So snail! I see you've learned to speak,
and question all ze things we do...
and zen you 'ave ze bloody cheek
to wonder why we're eating you?

You treat our gardens as your own,
you leave no 'laitue' left for us,
and act surprised if we zen choose
to serve you with asparagus?

And now you're telling us to stop?
Well sacré bleu! Zis man says 'no!'
I'll be 'le mort' before I take
instructions from an 'escargot.'

We're es-car-gone, mate. By the way,
your 'cordon bleu' is overrated.
We're heading back to Britain, where
we're slightly *less* appreciated.

Though there we're seen as garden pests,
and run right out of town...
at least they don't send white-clad men
with whisks, to hunt us down.

I'll take my chance at Mr. Smith's
allotment down in Norwich,
instead of sleeping in Toulouse
and waking up as porridge.

You snails are fools. Why not be here,
and part of something great –
instead of being hated zere?
Your place is on our plate.

And even if you all should leave
with lifts out of Dunkerque,
we'd hire ze Brits to hunt you down!
(I hear zey need ze work.)

Yes, face ze facts, you're meaningless
unless you're in a quiche.
If I was small and slimy, death
would come as a relief.

Fair enough then, Frenchie!
Perhaps we *will* all stay.
We'll hang about in 'gay Parie,'
we'll do just as you say.

We'll slither up the Eiffel Tower,
go swimming in the Seine,
and sure enough, a few of us
might wind up in cafés...

But as the British know full well,
we've mouths, to tear and chew.
So sleep with one eye open, Frogs
or we'll be eating YOU.

The Copper Wire

or, 'An Attempt to Tip the Snails'

'Snails are the natural enemy of the Delphinium...
when dealing with these creatures, your goal should be
eradication.'

- Display at Country Show

To whom it may concern –
plants do *not* feel pain.
'Man is the natural enemy of the carrot'
would be a stupid thing to say,
so why us? Why all this vilification,
of simple, devout vegetarians?

All day I see gardeners (cruel Mr. McGregor)
laying lengths of copper wire
around our lunch – to stop our hearts –
to end our innocent existence,
submerged in soil like landmines. Hidden.
Have you fiends never read the Geneva convention?

This is war. We gave your peas a chance,
withdrew our shell-shocked troops from France
(de Gaulle, I have some news for you,
that wasn't a grenade you threw...)
but still you let the practice
of mass snailicide continue. Let's talk pellets.
Those mute blue specks of death
which aim to take away our breath
and send our brother/sisters up to heaven –
are ending lives already brief,
and *still* misspent avoiding beaks
or dodging feet (see also, page eleven).

We're sure beer-baths would do for *you*
if we made some of human size,
but we're not ones to waste our lives
(though they are used for slug suicides).

We need no salt on our salad,
yet you still feel compelled to provide.

This is no joke. I've seen websites,
magazine spreads – *books* – which advocate
'stomping' on us. 'Throw them in the street!
That works!' You cry, and still
your mission's not complete. In gardens
words like 'lures' are often spoken,
you bring methaldyhde-based poisons,
predatory *devil-snails* in to devour us...
That thin copper wire in the topsoil
separates man from beast –
but which is which? When one side sits
and types up *murderous suggestions*,
while the other cowers under leaves?
But no-one asks the question.

So it escalates. We fight dirty, too.
Ever seen a brand new carpet raked with slime?
I have. And one day you'll find out
why they call a group of snails a 'rout'...
We'll ignore the weeds and nettles, go
for the brightest, most *expensive* growth;
catch coaches down to garden shows.
Mankind, you brought this on yourselves.

And so both sides despair. Dear human reader,
I write this not to point the finger,
apportion blame, or make a threat.
I'm sure that (as in all great fights)
both sides just want the war to end,
so I've written this missive in English
to *humanise* us. Show we could be friends.

Our own generosity stuns us. We'll be waiting
by the post box, should you wish to meet.
And before you turn us down, consider
how this time will be noted in history –
that you sought our utter destruction,
while snail-kind wished only to eat.

And if it should happen that you don't believe us,
remember who writes down this history.

VICTORS.

Snail's Sense of Self

National Poetry Day, 2010. Official theme: 'Home'

Home? I myself am home,
either way I turn is home.
Anywhere I lay my head.

I am under no illusions.
I am not the jaguar,
no tiger, burning bright;
not the fuzzy squirrel,
not the cruel black crow.
In the ring-fight of the animals
I would be among the first to go.

I am not a good mascot,
certainly no fashion statement.
Can't do a day's honest graft.
I won't keep the rats at bay,
or the flies. Can't fetch a stick,
or lead the blind. My song,
on tape, will not relax you,
I have no star sign.

I inspire no cartoon antics,
no-one wants me for their pet;
try, and you will fail
to have a snail
seen at the vet.

I am no lovesick swan, or penguin,
I barely even have a sex.

But there must be a place for me,
o traveller of the pavements,
of the hedgerows, over nations –
although it takes a while –
a place for one who'll happily pack
his troubles up, and smile.

I *am* the stuff of poetry.
We all are, in the end.
Just keep me in your heart,
your works of art,
I'll be your friend.

Slug Goes to Rehab

Snail told our Slug to go to rehab,
he said 'yes, fine, yes.'
Slug took himself along to rehab,
and this is what they said:

'Your blood sugar is much too low,
your liver's in a state.
Your hair no longer wants to grow,
and you've put on lots of weight.'

'I've no regrets,' says Slug.

'You've got a dozen STIs,
you're wanted by police.
There's a funny smell about your slime,
and your skin's become all creased.'

'I've no regrets,' says Slug.

'But...
the vet wants me to put you down,
your mother hopes he does!
Your father said he was concerned,
but I'm not convinced he was.'

'I've no regrets,' says Slug.

The clinic gave him free advice,
he promptly disobeyed.
His head's now swelled to quite a size,
and has turned a funny shade.

'I've no regrets!' Says Slug.

('I wo we web,' he really said,
the swelling impairing his speech.)

Now Slug thinks back on all his woes,
upturned in someone's flowers.
Attended to, until he goes
(though now, we're talking hours).

A nurse hands him a pad and pen,
he gratefully accepts.
And in the centre, once again,
he writes: 'I've no regrets.'

    'Except...'

A Snail's Pace

Slower than the motion
of an oceanic plate –
Confucius say: 'man who employs snail
must learn to wait'

must learn to put away his watch,
and find a different pace.

Your man must learn
this life which we are leading
is no race –

for snail has much to teach him,
before man can be great.

Snail's Postcard from Heaven

You'll be searching through your 'snail mail',
and wondering who this postcard's from;
the blank, no-name-been-given one...

So let me tell you. Yes, it's me,
the snail that you once stood on.

And the postcard isn't blank, it's just
the god of snails' almighty light,
screwing with the contrast.

Anyway – how are you doing?
From my new celestial slithering grounds
(where lettuce comprises each surface)
I've kept a watchful eye on you
to see if my message sunk in.

And what did I see, on peering down?
You, churning out snail poetry.
Whether from guilt, or inspiration –
I don't know. But god got me a copy.

And frankly, I'm impressed!
You wrote me quite a handsome legacy.
It seems I've managed more by death
(and haunting) than mum dreamed for me.

So now? I'm just relaxing, mostly.
Reading through your verse, quite happy,
having a snail of a time. Except,
I feel the book needs one more thing...
I've spotted an omission.

So I thought I'd send this postcard,
for inclusion in the next edition.

I'm having far more fun up here
than I could if I was living,
so rest your pen, J.M. And yes –
my friend, *you are forgiven*.